Christmas Gifts

Valerie Howard

Copyright © 2015 by Valerie Howard
Christmas Gifts By Valerie Howard

Printed in the United States of America
ISBN 978-1516964383

Cast of Characters:

Principal Kingsly: adult woman (17 lines)

Teacher (voice only): adult man or woman (1 line)

Ben: older kid, new kid in school (30 lines)

Melody: girl Ben's age (6 lines)

Stephanie: girl Ben's age (5 lines)

Alex: boy Ben's age (6 lines)

David: boy Ben's age (17 lines)

Cindy: younger girl (2 lines)

Mandy: younger girl (1 line)

Kid #1 (1 line)

Kid #2 (1 line)

Kid #3 (1 line)

Scene I

In an auditorium with metal chairs or students (of all ages) standing and facing the principal for morning announcements.

Principal Kingsly: Good morning, students.

All Students: Good morning, Principal Kingsly.

Kingsly: I trust all of you had a safe and happy weekend and are ready to get back into the swing of things this morning!

Students groan, yawn, roll eyes, make faces, mumble, sound less than enthusiastic, etc.

Kingsly: Okay. Well, I have some news that may wake all of you up. It's time to start preparing for our annual Christmas Talent Show!

Students act excited, give high fives, say things like, "Yes!" "Awesome!" "I know what I'm going to do!" David looks disinterested and crosses his arms and slouches.

Kingsly: Now, I want every student in this school to come up with something to do to help with the show. This year's theme is "What Christmas Means to Me," and I want everyone to try to figure out how they can show our audience the true meaning of Christmas. God has gifted each one of you in a special and unique way, and I want you to use your talents in the show. Be thinking about what you can do.

Cindy *(raises hand and Principal Kingsly points to her)*: Can we sing a song?

Kingsly: Singing a song would be a great idea, Cindy. Now, the show isn't for three weeks, so you all have time to think about your part, but since it's fresh on your minds now, I'm going to give you a few minutes to discuss this among yourselves and sign up for a talent on the board before going to your classrooms.

Students break into smaller groups, some go up to the principal and sign up for talents. Melody, Stephanie, Alex, and Ben take center stage.

Alex: Ben, what are you going to do for the talent show? You're new this year, so if you need any help with your act, just let us know.

Ben: I have no idea what I can do. What kinds of things do the kids usually sign up for?

Melody: Well, Alex usually recites some verses. Mandy usually reads a short story or poem she wrote. Stephanie usually helps her mom with refreshments. The younger grades usually get together and sing a song. And David usually skips the show because he's "sick" *(uses air quotes)* or something.

Ben: Wow, I don't think I can do anything like that. I can't sing or memorize lines or write poems. Last time I tried to memorize a Bible verse at church, it was a disaster. Maybe I'll just help clean up after the show.

Stephanie *(looking at sign-up board)*: Looks like you're too late. Billy and Cody already signed up to set up and clean up. Principal Kingsly won't let more than two kids sign up for those.

Ben: Great. Now what am I supposed to do?

Kingsly: All right students, your time is up. Everyone get to your classrooms, and we'll begin our day.

Students groan and exit.
Lights fade.
Curtain closes.

Scene II

Bell rings. Lights on.

Teacher: *(from off stage)* And don't forget to read the next two chapters for homework. Have a good evening, and I will see you all tomorrow morning.

Melody, Stephanie, Alex, Ben, and David enter stage with backpacks/jackets/ready to go home.

Alex: Hey, David, are you going to do anything for the talent show this year?

David: Drop it, Alex. I never do anything for the talent show, remember? I wouldn't even be in this dumb school if I had any other option. So why don't you just leave me alone and go memorize your Bible passages and impress everyone with your giant brain? *(Exits.)*

Alex: *(calling after David)* Okay, sorry, just forget I said anything. *(To rest of group)* Wow, what's eating him?

Stephanie: Alex, you know David never comes to the talent show. I think he gets stage fright.

Melody: I think he's just being rude. It's not like Principal Kingsly is asking him to do something challenging. She'd be happy if he just blew up a few balloons to help decorate.

Ben: *(thoughtfully, looking at David's exit point)* Maybe he has the right idea. I can't think of a single thing that I can do for the show.

Stephanie: Do you get stage fright too?

Ben: *(shrugs)* I don't think so, I've never really done anything on stage before, so I don't really know.

Alex: You've never been in any plays, talent shows, or concerts before?

Ben: No. *(Rubs the back of his neck and looks a little embarrassed to admit this.)* I've never had the opportunity to do anything like this before.

Melody: Well, we have three weeks to figure it out. You'll think of something. C'mon, we'll help you right now! *(Motions for other kids to join them on stage.)*

Kids toss books, backpack, jackets to the side, all other kids join them onstage.

Kid #1 *(handing Ben three small balls)***:** I have an idea. Try to juggle these.

Ben: Okay. *(Tries to juggle a few times, drops balls everywhere, gets frustrated, hands balls back to Kid #1.)* Sorry, not happening.

Kid #2: What about dancing? *(Turns on CD player for some music.)*

Ben: *(Tries to dance, but falls down and grabs his ankle as if in pain. Stays sitting in the middle of the stage.)* Ouch! I don't think that's going to work either. This is a waste of time, guys, sorry.

Melody: Wait a minute, we haven't tried everything yet. Here, how about we all sing a song, and Ben, you can listen and try to join in when you feel comfortable, okay?

Ben: *(shrugs)* I guess I can try.

Kids sing Angels We Have Heard on High.
Ben doesn't sing.

Angels We Have Heard on High
Translated by James Chadwick

Angels we have heard on high,
Sweetly singing o'er the plains.
And the mountains in reply
Echoing their joyous strains.

Gloria, in excelsis Deo! Gloria, in excelsis Deo!

Shepherds, why this jubilee?
Why your joyous strains prolong?
What the gladsome tidings be
Which inspire your heavenly song?

Gloria, in excelsis Deo! Gloria, in excelsis Deo!

Come to Bethlehem and see
Him Whose birth the angels sing;
Come, adore on bended knee,
Christ the Lord, the newborn King.

Gloria, in excelsis Deo! Gloria, in excelsis Deo!

See Him in a manger laid
Jesus Lord of heaven and earth;
Mary, Joseph, lend your aid,
With us sing our Savior's birth.

Gloria, in excelsis Deo! Gloria, in excelsis Deo!

Mandy: You can sing that, can't you?

Ben: I don't know...

Cindy: C'mon, just try it. We won't laugh.

Ben *(hesitantly)***:** Okay. *(Sings "Glo-o-o-o-oria" very quietly.)*

Kid #3: Louder!

Ben: *(Sings louder, but horribly and very off-key, voice cracking. Other kids just look wide-eyed and horrified, some maybe cover their mouths, some drop their jaws, but no one laughs. He stops and shakes his head.)* Oh, what's the use? I can't sing either! I'm sorry, everybody. Thanks for trying to help me, but maybe God just didn't give me any special talents after all. I'm just not good at anything. I gotta go home. *(Ben grabs his backpack and exits.)*

Other kids look sad and start collecting their school things to head home and start moping off the stage.

Stephanie: Don't worry guys, if he still wants to be a part of the show, we'll help him figure out what to do, you'll see.

Lights fade.
Curtains down.

Scene III

In a classroom at school.

Kingsly: Hello, children. Just popping in to remind you that there is only one week left until the talent show! Those of you who haven't signed up for anything yet, please do so soon. *(Looks at watch.)* It's time for lunch now, so go ahead to the cafeteria. David and Ben, please see me before heading out the door.

David and Ben approach Principal Kingsly while the rest of the kids file off stage in a line.

Kingsly: Do you two plan on participating in the show next week?

David: Nope!

Kingsly: All right, David, you may go to lunch.

David exits.

Kingsly: And Ben? What about you?

Ben: I want to, but I've been having a tough time thinking of what I could do. It doesn't seem like I'm good at anything. I just don't want to make a fool out of myself in front of everyone.

Kingsly: I see. Well, Ben, God has made you a unique person, and He's gifted you with certain talents and abilities so you can serve Him. You might have to think outside the box, and you certainly aren't required to do something on the stage if you aren't gifted that way, but try to think of some way you can help out with the show, and I will make sure your talents– whatever they may be– are put to use.

Ben: Okay, thank you, I'll keep thinking.

Kingsly exits.

David returns with a lunch box and looks surprised to see Ben still in the room. He goes to a chair and starts eating. Ben watches him.

David: Got a staring problem?

Ben: Staring problem? No, sorry. I was just wondering why you're eating in here instead of out in the cafeteria with everyone else. Aren't they nice to you?

David *(scoffs)***:** Yeah, everyone's nice. Too nice.

Ben *(confused)***:** Too nice?

David: You wouldn't understand. You're one of them.

Ben: One of them?

David: What are you, a parrot? *(sighs)* Not that it's any of your business, but if you haven't figured it out yet, I'm not exactly like the other kids here. I don't even believe in God. I just come to this school because my mom got religious after her and Dad split up, and she gave me no choice. All those "goody-two-shoes" talking at once makes me– *(waves his hand dismissively)* Aww, never mind, you don't get it.

Ben: I understand more than you think.

David: Yeah, right.

Ben: No, really. You want to know why my parents home schooled me for all these years?

David shrugs and keeps looking at his food.

Ben: I'll tell you why. It's because I was so full of anger until I was eleven, I kept getting into fistfights, and my parents tried to keep me away from anyone I might hurt.

David: Now you're just making stuff up.

Ben: You think so, huh? Do you see this scar? Right here? *(Rolls up shirt sleeve and points to forearm and indicates long scar with a wave of his hand.)* That's a third degree burn from two years ago. You wanna know how I got it?

David: Roasting marshmallows over a campfire while singing Kumbaya?

Ben: No...I set my Dad's shed on fire after we had a big argument.

David *(rolls his eyes in an exaggerated way)***:** Now you're really making stuff up.

Ben *(shrugs)***:** Feel free to look it up. I'm sure the article is still on the internet, and the police report is probably still at my house somewhere, I can bring it in tomorrow if you need me to prove it.

David: He called the cops on you?

Ben: Yeah. Said it was for my own good. I spent two months in the juvenile detention center.

David: So, that's what straightened you out and made you all about God now?

Ben *(laughs)***:** Not even a little bit.

David: So what was it?

Ben: It was my Dad. For the two months I was gone, he rebuilt the shed by himself. And he took the time to write me a letter every day. Because of my behavior at the detention center, I was never allowed to get my mail until my sentence was up, so I didn't know about the letters until I was released. On my way out the door, they handed me my belongings and sixty-one envelopes. I read every word on the ride home. All of them told me that my Dad loved me, had forgiven me and God loved me and could forgive me too. Because of Jesus' sacrifice on the cross, all my sins had been paid for, if I'd just put my faith in Him.

David *(skeptical)*: And just like that *(snaps his fingers)*, you changed?

Ben: Well, I didn't become a "goody-two shoes" overnight, no. But when I turned to God and told Him I was sorry for sinning against Him, and that I believed Jesus died for me, the change in my heart was instant.

David *(crumpling up his trash, standing up while grabbing lunch tray)*: Huh. Nice story. I'm going to go shoot some hoops before class starts. See ya. *(Exits.)*

Melody, Stephanie, and Alex enter from opposite side.

Melody: Wow, Ben! That was great!

Ben: What? Lunch?

Alex: No, the way you just talked to David about how God changed you.

Stephanie: He's never let anyone talk to him about anything "religious" before.

Ben *(shrugs)*: I was just talking. No big deal.

Melody: Hey, that gives me an idea. Come on!

Kids exit.
Lights fade.
Curtains close.

Scene IV

Talent show set. Microphones, risers, instruments on stage, etc.

Kingsly: Good evening, parents, grandparents, aunts, uncles, and friends! Welcome to our eighth annual Christmas Talent Show!

(Applause.)

Kingsly: We will start with Mandy Evans presenting a poem she wrote all by herself entitled "The Meaning of Christmas."

(Applause. Mandy enters, Kingsly exits.)

Mandy *(reading or reciting)*:
C is for Christ, sent down from above.
H for His heart that's full of love.
R for the righteous life He'd live.
I for iniquity He would forgive.
S for the sinners His spilt blood bought
T for the tomb where His body was brought.
M for a miracle, He rose from the dead.
A for ascension, He went on ahead.
S for salvation, leaving out none
Who trust in the work of God's own Son.

(Applause. Mandy exits, Kingsly enters.)

Kingsly *(applauding)*: Great job, Mandy! Now, I'd like to take a moment to introduce our students presenting talents off-stage this evening. Sarah and Missy decorated the auditorium. Billy and Cody will clean up after the show, and Stephanie, with her mother's help, set up a table of refreshments in the back for after the show. Let's give a big round of applause for our behind-the-scenes talents tonight.

(Applause.)

Kingsly: Next, we have Alex Morris reciting the Christmas story from Luke chapter two! *(Claps and exits.)*

(Alex enters center stage and recites Luke 2:1-18.)

(Applause as Alex exits and Kingsly enters.)

Kingsly *(clapping)***:** Thank you, Alex! Very well done! Next, we have some students from the younger grades singing O Holy Night.

(Applause as Cindy and some younger girls and boys enter the stage and Kingsly exits.)

Cindy and friends sing O Holy Night.

O Holy Night
by John Sullivan Dwight

O holy night, the stars are brightly shining.
It is the night of our dear Savior's birth.
Long lay the world in sin and error pining
Till he appeared and the soul felt its worth.
The thrill of hope, the weary world rejoices,
For yonder breaks a new and glorious morn.

Fall on your knees! O hear the angel voices!
O night divine! O night when Christ was born!
O night, O holy night, O night divine!

Led by the light of faith serenely beaming,
With glowing hearts by His cradle we stand.
So led by a light of a star sweetly gleaming,
Here came the wise men from Orient land.
The King of kings lay thus in lowly manger;
In all our trials born to be our Friend.

He knows our need, to our weakness is no stranger,
Behold your King! Before him lowly bend!
Behold your King! Before him lowly bend!

Truly He taught us to love one another,
His law is love and His gospel is peace.
Chains shall He break, for the slave is our brother.
And in His name all oppression shall cease.
Sweet hymns of joy in grateful chorus raise we,
Let all within us praise His holy name.

Christ is the Lord! Oh praise His name forever,
His power and glory ever more proclaim!
His power and glory ever more proclaim!

(Applause as Cindy and friends exit and Kingsly enters.)

Kingsly: Well done, ladies! We only have one talent presentation left before our school Christmas song, so please welcome our school's newest student, Ben Robinson!

(Applause as Kingsly exits and Ben enters.)

Ben *(unfolds piece of paper)*: I wasn't sure what I was going to do for the show tonight because I wasn't sure that God had made me good at anything. I used to be really good at breaking the rules, but other than that, I didn't think I had been gifted with anything special. Then my friends helped me discover that God had given me something. He'd given me a changed heart. And that's what I'd like to share with you tonight.

(Starts reading paper.)

When I was younger, Christmas just meant a vacation from school and getting new video games. It was just a day where I acted greedy and selfish, and angry if I didn't get exactly what I wanted. All of that changed once I realized Christmas was about God Himself coming down to our little world as a tiny baby.

But, that's not all He did. The story doesn't stop in Bethlehem. God's Son, Jesus, lived a perfect life. Because He was God, He couldn't do anything sinful or wrong. Then, people who hated Him for telling the truth put Him to death on a cross.

But the story doesn't stop in the grave, either. Three days later, Jesus proved that He was God by conquering death and stepping out of the tomb that held Him. He had paid for all of our sins with His sacrifice. God had poured out His wrath on His Son instead of on the one who really deserved the punishment – me.

Once I realized God's forgiveness could be mine, no matter how many bad things I had done, I prayed and asked Jesus to save me. Now Christmas has a new meaning. Now Christmas is a reminder of God's patience toward me and His undeserved forgiveness for all my sins.

(Folds paper.)

Thank you.

(Applause while Ben exits the stage and Kingsly enters.)

Kingsly: Thank you for sharing that with us, Ben. Very heartwarming. And last, but not least, we ask all the studen–

David *(running to the stage from the back of the audience)*: Wait! Wait! *(Whispers something to Principal Kingsly when he reaches her.)*

Kingsly *(side eyed and nodding)*: All right. Everyone, this is David Price, and he will be introducing our final performance this evening.

David: I'd like to introduce this year's song by saying that I never understood the real meaning of Christmas until hearing Ben talk tonight, but I get it now. I've decided to put my faith in Jesus, and I believe He is my Savior. Now that my sins have been forgiven, I can't think of a better way to celebrate this holiday than by joining in our school's Christmas song for the first time. We will be singing "What Christmas Means to Me." *(All kids join him on stage in concert formation. Music begins.)*

Sing What Christmas Means to Me.

What Christmas Means to Me
by Valerie Howard

(Sing to the tune of: It Came Upon a Midnight Clear)

Some think that Christmas is all about the people that they love.
But they forget about the One God sent from up above.
Some think perhaps it's nothing more than parties, gifts, and fun.
But they don't know the price it cost God's precious, only Son.

If Christmas has a meaning, then whatever can it be?
Listen, and I'll tell you now what Christmas means to me.
It means Christ came to live perfectly and die upon a tree.
It means He rose so we can be free, when we truly believe.

Even though we were born in sin, God's love has made a way.
Christ came down to the Earth one night, slept in a bed of hay.
The story did not end that night in starry Bethlehem.
As Jesus grew, He always knew He'd die for all of man.

If Christmas has a meaning, then whatever can it be?
Listen, and I'll tell you now what Christmas means to me.
It means Christ came to live perfectly and die upon a tree.
It means He rose so we can be free, when we truly believe.

Kingsly joins children on stage.
Everyone bows.
Curtains close.
Lights fade.

Props:

Scene I:
Sign up board
Backpacks

Scene II:
Backpacks
Jackets
Books
CD player
Juggling balls

Scene III:
Desks
Lunch tray
Basketball (optional)

Scene IV:
Microphones
Risers (optional)
Piece of paper for Ben

Costumes:

In scenes I through III, children and Principal Kingsly are dressed for school. School uniforms or jeans and T-shirts are both appropriate costumes.

In scene IV, children are dressed up as if they are in a talent show. They may wear the same clothes they've been wearing throughout, or they may perform a quick wardrobe change after scene III.

Variations:

For fewer cast members:

Cindy (or Mandy) and Kid #1, #2, and #3 may all be played by the same person.

Principal Kingsly may disguise voice as the teacher calling off stage.

If you enjoyed this play, you might also like ...

Christmas Lights by Valerie Howard

No Time For Christmas by Valerie Howard

Christmas Catastrophe by Steve and Valerie Howard

The Worst Christmas Ever by Elizabeth Rowe and Juliet Rowe

Find books for children, teens, and adults at
www.AuthorValerieHoward.com

Follow what's new at
www.Facebook.com/ValerieHowardBooks

Made in the USA
Monee, IL
06 October 2022

15355374R00015